THE BATHROOM GAME BOOK

by

Russ Edwards & Jack Kreismer

RED-LETTER PRESS, INC.
Saddle River, New Jersey

ACKNOWLEDGMENTS

Project Development Coordinator:
Kobus Reyneke

Cover design and typography:
s.w.artz, inc.

Editorial:
Jeff Kreismer

Significant Others:
Theresa Adragna
Kathy Hoyt, Robin Kreismer
Jim & Rory Tomlinson, Lori Walsh

INTRODUCTION

For more than twenty years, the original Bathroom Library has entertained people on the go everywhere. With millions of copies out there, it proves that we're not all wet about bathroom reading.

Now, as heir to the throne, we proudly introduce a brand new Bathroom Library. We hope you enjoy this installment of it.

Yours flushingly,

Jack Kreismer
Publisher

FOR AMERICA'S
FAVORITE READING ROOM

THE
BATHROOM
GAME BOOK

*Brain Teasers To
Keep You On
The Edge of Your Seat*

THE BATHROOM LIBRARY

RED-LETTER PRESS, INC.
Saddle River, New Jersey

INITIALLY SPEAKING

In this quiz the number on the left is based upon the first letters for words which are provided on the right.

Example: 4 = Q. in a G. (Quarts in a Gallon)

1. 26 = L. in the A.

2. 3,600 = S. in an H.

3. 54 = C. in the D. (with the J.)

4. 9 = L. of a C.

5. 12 = S. of the Z.

6. 3 = M. in a T.

7. 20,000 = L.U. the S.

8. 13 = O.C.

9. 60 = M. in an H.

10. 12 = D. of C.

GAMES PEOPLE PLAY

How many hearts are there on the 6 of hearts?

8.

ANSWERS

1. 26 = Letters in the Alphabet.

2. 3,600 = Seconds in an Hour.

3. 54 = Cards in the Deck (with the Jokers).

4. 9 = Lives of a Cat.

5. 12 = Signs of the Zodiac.

6. 3 = Men in a Tub.

7. 20,000 = Leagues Under the Sea.

8. 13 = Original Colonies.

9. 60 = Minutes in an Hour.

10. 12 = Days of Christmas.

GAMES PEOPLE PLAY

What are the dots on a pair of dice called?

Pips.

PHRASE CRAZE

*Try to decipher the meaning of the following,
keeping in mind the placement of the words.*

Example: $\frac{EGGS}{EASY}$ is eggs over easy.

1. FRIENDJUSTFRIEND

2. SYMPHON

3. OFFENSE

4. OHOLENE

5. SHkeepAPE

6. weather
   feeling

7. ALLworld

8. PLATE
   E
   T
   S

9. ENDSSDNE

10. Gun Jr.

GAMES PEOPLE PLAY

In England it's called draughts. In America it's called …?

Checkers

ANSWERS

1. Just between friends.

2. Unfinished symphony.

3. Capital offense.

4. Hole in one.

5. Keep in shape.

6. Feeling under the weather.

7. It's a small world after all.

8. Step up to the plate.

9. Making ends meet.

10. Son of a gun!

GAMES PEOPLE PLAY
(ON OTHER PEOPLE)

At a restaurant, ask the waitress if you can have a seat for your "imaginary friend." … Hey, and when you've finished your dinner make sure to pay in pennies.

WHAT ARE THE ODDS?

Which is the odd one out and why?

1. a) Cocker Spaniel b) Siamese c) Boxer d) Golden Retriever
   Hint: Type.

2. a) New York b) Boston c) Miami d) San Francisco
   Hint: Location.

3. a) 2 b) 4 c) 9 d) 16
   Hint: Multiples.

4. a) Roger Maris b) Mickey Mantle c) Hank Aaron d) Barry Bonds
   Hint: 50.

5. a) Sonny Bono b) Ronald Reagan c) Clint Eastwood
   d) Tom Hanks
   Hint: Donkeys and elephants.

6. a) *Newsweek* b) *Sports Illustrated* c) *Time* d) *Reader's Digest*
   Hint: Time.

7. a) Peter Jennings b) David Brinkley c) Walter Cronkite
   d) Mike Wallace
   Hint: Anchors away.

8. a) pip b) radar c) mare d) peep
   Hint: Letter perfect.

9. a) *Easy Rider* b) *One Flew Over the Cuckoo's Nest*
   c) *Chinatown* d) *A Few Good Men*
   Hint: Sorry, Jacks are not wild here.

10. a) Vanessa Williams b) Katie Harman c) Phyllis George
    d) Bess Myerson
    Hint: No crowning glory here.

ANSWERS

1. B ... Siamese is the only one that's not a breed of dogs.

2. D ... All the other cities are on the east coast.

3. A ... All the others are perfect squares.

4. C ... Aaron's the only one who didn't hit at least 50 homers in a season.

5. D ... Hanks is the only actor who didn't become a politician.

6. D ... It's the only one that's a monthly rather than a weekly periodical.

7. D ... Wallace is the only one who wasn't a network tv news anchor.

8. C ... It's the only word that's not a palindrome.

9. B ... The film is the only one of the four for which Jack Nicholson won an Oscar. (Of course, he has won others.)

10. A ... She was the only one to be stripped of her Miss America title.

GAMES PEOPLE PLAY

What company introduced its product in 1949
and first called it Automatic Binding Bricks?

Lego.

ARKANSAS SMITH

Swashbuckling adventurer-scientist, Arkansas Smith had made what he felt was the find of a lifetime. His search had taken him all around the world and he had spent the last year dodging Nazis in Egypt, devil-worshippers in India, headhunters in South America and condo salesmen in Florida.

As the tramp steamer carrying him and his precious cargo pulled into New York Harbor, he realized he had only a short time to make the monthly meeting of The Explorer's Club and spring his surprise on his sniping colleagues.

Lacking any time to make himself presentable, he caught a cab to the Club, rushed past the doorman and up to the stage where he unveiled his find. It was an ancient clay tablet, inscribed with the date 215 B.C. and purporting to be an account of the last days of Atlantis, written as the continent heaved and shuddered and finally slipped beneath the sea forever.

Instead of expected admiration, however, he received nothing but contempt and was summarily tossed out into the street. As the dust settled back on his hat, he realized what he had missed in his former excitement. What was it?

GAMES PEOPLE PLAY

According to Hoyle, what are the
"oldest gaming implements known to man?"

Dice.

ANSWER

How could an ancient scribe write something and date it B.C.? How could they know that in the future there'd be a B.C. and an A.D.? It had to be a hoax.

GAMES PEOPLE PLAY

Illinois Avenue is the most landed upon space in Monopoly. What's second?

According to Irvin R. Hentzel of Iowa State University it's "Go." The mathematician used a computer to figure out the probability of landing on each square. Rounding out the top ten, in order, are B.&O. Railroad, Free Parking, Tennessee Avenue, New York Avenue, Reading Railroad, St. James Place, Water Works and Pennsylvania Railroad.

MISCELLANEOUS MINDBENDERS

1. What goes around the world and stays in a corner?

2. A man pushed and pushed his car past various hotels. He stopped when he reached a certain hotel and realized he was bankrupt. Why?

3. What's in the middle of nowhere?

4. Add three letters to make the following complete: TNESSFF_ _ _.

5. Seven pieces of coal, a carrot and a scarf are lying on little Johnny's front yard. No one, including Johnny, had put them on the lawn yet there's a plausible reason why they should be there. Do you know it?

6. What is it that's more powerful than God, more evil than the devil, the rich don't have it, the poor do, and if you eat it you will die?

7. Answer this quick riddle/rhyme. What is it of a bird that's not in the sky, yet can swim in the water and remain dry?

8. She's your uncle's sister but she isn't legally your aunt. Who can she be?

9. An electric train is travelling northeast at 80 miles per hour. The wind is blowing southerly at 20 miles per hour. Do you know in what direction the smoke from the engine will blow?

10. Tom's mother had three children. One was named Penny and another named Nickel. What was the name of the third child?

ANSWERS

1. A postage stamp.

2. He was playing Monopoly.

3. The letter "h."

4. TTO completes the countdown from ten to one.

5. Johnny had made a snowman and, eventually, it melted.

6. Nothing.

7. Its shadow.

8. Your mother.

9. Smoke doesn't blow from an electric engine.

10. Tom, of course.

GAMES PEOPLE PLAY

(ON OTHER PEOPLE)

Here's one for your answering machine.
Make a recording where you say, "Hello." Then wait a few
seconds and say, "Hello" a little bit louder. Wait a few
seconds and say, "That's better. I'm sorry, we're not
available right now, ya-da-ya-da-ya-da."

ONCE REMOVED

Change each pair of words into synonyms by
moving one letter from one word and placing it into the other.

1. tine and bid

2. aid and scour

3. oak and west

4. potion and pierce

5. age and ranger

6. flit and croquet

7. shear and car

8. spiny and grate

9. lave and quite

10. fog and bleat

GAMES PEOPLE PLAY

What's the name of the rich uncle
in the game of Monopoly?

Milburn Pennybags.

ANSWERS

1. tie and bind.

2. acid and sour.

3. soak and wet.

4. portion and piece.

5. rage and anger.

6. flirt and coquet.

7. sear and char.

8. spin and gyrate.

9. leave and quit.

10. flog and beat.

GAMES PEOPLE PLAY

Which game was introduced first -
Go to the Head of the Class or Candy Land?

*Go to the Head of the Class, in 1938 ...
Candy Land was first issued in 1949.*

EASY DOES IT

Here's an obviously simple quiz with some not so obvious answers.

1. Which can see better in total darkness - an owl, a raccoon or a skunk?

2. Suppose that 14% of the people in Detroit, Michigan, have unlisted telephone numbers. Now suppose you randomly pick 200 names from the phone book for that city. Assuming that the 14% figure holds true, how many of those names you've selected will have unlisted numbers?

3. What month has 28 days?

4. How many times can one be subtracted from one hundred?

5. If your doctor gave you three pills and told you to take one every half hour, how long would they last?

6. A shepherd had seventeen sheep. All but seven died. How many did he have left?

7. Take two oranges from three oranges and what do you have?

8. How many animals of each species did Moses take aboard the ark?

9. If you entered a dark room with only one match and you knew that in the room there were a kerosene lamp, an oil stove and a cigarette, which would you light first?

10. Is there a fourth of July in England?

ANSWERS

1. No animal can see in total darkness.

2. None will be unlisted.

3. All of them.

4. Only once.

5. One hour.

6. Seven, of course.

7. Two oranges.

8. None ... It was Noah who had the ark.

9. The match.

10. Yes ... There's a fourth of July everywhere.

GAMES PEOPLE PLAY

In Monopoly, how many bills does each player get
to begin the game?

27 ... five $1, $5 and $10 bills; two $50s,
$100s and $500s; and six $20s.

FIVE EASY PIECES

*The following ten letter words have been chopped up
into five 2 letter chunks. See if you can re as se mb le them.*

1. IT PE ER TY WR

2. SV ER AN SE TR

3. CT RY DI NA IO

4. CI TI AR AL FI

5. CC ES UL SU SF

6. IT ON IN TI IA

7. TI DI AD AL ON

8. GA ON OB TI LI

9. IB ED IN LE CR

10. NA FI ER IL NG

GAMES PEOPLE PLAY

Can you name the game that was developed from the
Italian lotto game Tombola in 1880?

Bingo.

ANSWERS

1. Typewriter.

2. Transverse.

3. Dictionary.

4. Artificial.

5. Successful.

6. Initiation.

7. Additional.

8. Obligation.

9. Incredible.

10. Fingernail.

GAMES PEOPLE PLAY

"Small bowls" was a popular game among the likes of
George Washington, Thomas Jefferson and John Adams.
By what name do we know "small bowls" today?

Marbles.

TIME AND TIME AGAIN

1. What is one-sixtieth of one-sixtieth of one-twenty-fourth of a day?

2. True or false: Any month that starts on a Sunday will have a Friday the 13th.

3. How long is the minute hand on "Big Ben?"
   a) 3 feet b) 5 feet c) 8 feet d) 11 feet

4. "Two days ago I was 69 years old. Next year, I'll be 72." How can someone make that statement?

5. What is the third hand on a clock called?

6. An extremely odd happenstance occurred in 1978 on the 6th of May at 12:34 p.m. Do you know what it was?

7. When is the only time (remember, we're talking time here) you can add five to eleven and have the solution be four?

8. If it were an hour later, it would be half as long 'til noon as it is now. If it were two hours earlier, it would be twice as long to noon as it is now. What time is it?

9. February is the shortest month of the year. What's the second shortest month?

10. What word, when written in capital letters, is the same spelled backwards, forwards, and upside down?

ANSWERS

1. One second.

2. True.

3. Strictly speaking, the answer is "none of the above." Big Ben is the bell inside the clock, not the clock itself. But if you answered "d", we'll give you credit.

4. This can only be said about someone who is born on December 31 and is saying that on January 1.

5. The second hand.

6. At that exact moment, the time read 12:34, 5/6/78.

7. If you were to tack on five hours to eleven o'clock, the time would be four o'clock.

8. 10 a.m.

9. April, when daylight savings time makes it a month which lasts 29 days and 23 hours.

10. NOON.

RUNNING NUMBERS

How many ...

1. Toes are there on a pig's foot?

2. Spaces are on a Monopoly board?

3. Children did the "Father of our country" have?

4. Black keys are there on a piano?

5. Words in the English language have 3 consecutive double-letters?

6. Laps are there in the Indianapolis 500?

7. Teams are there in college's "Big Ten?"

8. Holes are on a Chinese checkerboard?

9. Squares are on a Scrabble board?

10. Fingers does Mickey Mouse have?

GAMES PEOPLE PLAY

What game began in India
and was originally called Poona?

Badminton.

ANSWERS

1. 4.

2. 40.

3. George Washington had no children.

4. 36.

5. 1 - bookkeeper.

6. 200.

7. 11.

8. 121.

9. 225.

10. 8.

GAMES PEOPLE PLAY

The second best-selling board game in the world was
invented by Alfred M. Butts. Do you know it?

Scrabble.

YOU 'DA MAN!

See if you can solve these manly mindbogglers.

1. A man lives on the 20th floor of an apartment building. Every day he takes the elevator to the ground floor. When he returns, he takes it to the 10th floor and walks up the stairs to get to his apartment. Why?

2. A man went to a party, but stayed just briefly and only had a glass of punch. He was fortunate to be the first to drink it because everyone else who did died of poisoning. How come?

3. A man was bragging about his local softball team. He said, "Four of our men hit home runs and two of them were grand slams. We won 10 to 0 and not a single man crossed home plate." How could that be?

4. A man walks into a tavern and asks the bartender for a glass of water. The bartender pulls out a .45 and points the gun at the guy. The man says, "Thanks," and walks out. What happened?

5. A man gave his wife a bottomless receptacle which was eventually used to put her flesh and blood in. Can you be more precise as to what exactly it was that he gave her?

ANSWERS

1. He's not tall enough to reach the "20th floor" button so he presses number 10 and walks the remaining way.

2. Someone placed the poison in ice cubes. Because the man was an early-to-arrive and early-to-leave fellow, he drank the punch before the cubes melted.

3. They were all married.

4. The fellow had the hiccups and the bartender scared the daylights out of him and his problem.

5. A wedding ring.

GAMES PEOPLE PLAY

In chess, how many pieces does each player begin with?

16 ... A king, a queen, two knights,
two bishops, two castles and eight pawns.

COMMON SENSE

Try to find the common noun that fits with the other three.

Example: Bunk - Room - Twin   Answer: Bed

1. Tree - Drop - Meadowlark

2. Slipper - Eye - Shot

3. Easter - Dust- Bugs

4. Used - Side - Wash

5. Pound - Hot - Tired

6. Remover - Check - Ink

7. Fast - Form - Born

8. Dollar - Electric - Fold

9. Mate - Safety - Mark

10. Exercise - Radio - Computer

ANSWERS

1. Lemon.

2. Glass.

3. Bunny.

4. Car.

5. Dog.

6. Spot.

7. Free.

8. Bill.

9. Check.

10. Program.

GAMES PEOPLE PLAY

(ON OTHER PEOPLE)

Of course, we're the experts when it comes
to bathroom funny business. The next time
you're in a stall in a public restroom drop
a marble and cry out "Oh, no!! My glass eye!!"

ALL IN THE FAMILY

1. A lawyer and doctor were standing on line at the supermarket. One of them was the father of the other's son. Can you explain?

2. Is it possible for a man to have been married to his widow's sister?

3. When you're describing a pair of twins, how many people are you talking about?

4. A man and his sister were walking in the park one day when the man pointed to a boy and said, "There's my nephew." His sister said, "That's right, but he's not my nephew." How come?

5. Michael has twice as many brothers as he has sisters. His sister Judy has five times as many brothers as she has sisters. How many brothers and sister are in the family?

6. Jennifer and Lori were born on the same day. They have the same parents. They are sisters - but they are not twins. How can this be?

7. The man married the little boy's mother, but was not his father (in any step of the way). Who was he?

8. Why would you doubt this young woman's story? "My mother dreamed that she was drowning and became so frightened that she died of a heart attack in her sleep."

9. The 22nd and 24th presidents of the United States had the same mother and father, but were not brothers. Can you explain it?

10. Ralph's father is older than his grandfather. How can that be?

ANSWERS

1. They were husband and wife.

2. Sure ... If he married his wife's sister first.

3. Two ... A twin is one person. A pair of twins is like a pair of shoes.

4. It was the woman's son so the boy was her brother's nephew.

5. There are five boys and two girls.

6. They are two of a set of triplets (or more).

7. The clergyman.

8. No one would know what a dying woman was dreaming.

9. They were the same man, Grover Cleveland ... He served two terms as president, but they were not consecutive.

10. Ralph's father is older than his *maternal* grandfather.

MUSIC TO YOUR EARS

Can you identify the following song titles from the first letter of each word? We've given you a little bit of help by providing the performers.

1. HJ (Beatles)

2. WC (Bing Crosby)

3. CITW (Elton John)

4. PM (Billy Joel)

5. M (Jimmy Buffet)

6. VOL (Mariah Carey)

7. L (Eric Clapton)

8. R (Aretha Franklin)

9. TK (Faith Hill)

10. IWTS (Barry Manilow)

GAMES PEOPLE PLAY

Who was the original host of TV's Hollywood Squares?

Peter Marshall.

ANSWERS

1. *Hey, Jude!*

2. *White Christmas.*

3. *Candle in the Wind.*

4. *Piano Man.*

5. *Margaritaville.*

6. *Vision of Love.*

7. *Layla.*

8. *Respect.*

9. *This Kiss.*

10. *I Write The Songs.*

GAMES PEOPLE PLAY

Do you know the three one-eyed face cards
in a deck of cards?

*The king of diamonds, the jack of
hearts and the jack of spades.*

RODW CSRMABEL

Rearranged, the above spells "word scramble."
And that's just what we have here.
Complete the following joke by unscrambling the punch line.

Finister loved all the latest gadgets and so when the musical toilet seat came out he just had to have one. One day his wife's bridge club was at his house and the ladies took turns using the facilities.

The first lady came back all a-twitter and a-gog. "Oh, what a surprise! A musical toilet seat! Can you imagine that? It played Stardust for me!"

A few minutes later, another woman returned to the living room and reported that it played Beethoven's Fifth Symphony!

The latest in bathroom appliances was a huge hit as, one by one, the ladies tried it out.

Finally, it was Shirley's turn but she returned from the john none-too-pleased.

"What's wrong, Shirley? Didn't you like it?", asked a concerned Mrs. Finster.

"It's all right, I guess," answered Shirley hesitantly. "It's just that not only did I have to wait 'till last to use the bathroom, but as soon as I sat down it started playing...

1. HTE

2. RTSA

3. NLSAPDEG

4. NABNRE

ANSWER

1. THE

2. STAR

3. SPANGLED

4. BANNER.

GAMES PEOPLE PLAY

1. What would you be tossing if you were playing a game of Fourteen-Stop?

2. What shape is a Chinese Checkerboard?

3. The Unknown Comic was featured on what game show?

4. In the days of the Old West, what was a "California prayer book" to a gambler?

5. What's the first name of the inventor of Rubik's Cube?

5. Erno

4. A deck of cards

3. The Gong Show

2. It's a six-pointed star.

1. Darts

THE WORLD ACCORDING TO YOGI

All the vowels have been removed from these quotes from that master of malaprops and baseball Hall of Famer Yogi Berra. Replace them to complete the Yogi-ism.

1. "Whn y cm t th frk n th rd, tk t."

2. "Nnty prcnt f th gm s hlf mntl."

3. " nckl n't wrth dm nymr ."

4. " f ppl dn't wnt t cm t th bll prk, hw r y gnn stp thm?"

5. "Nbdy gs t tht rstrnt nymr . t's t crwdd."

6. " t gts lt rly t thr ."

7. " tk tw hr np ths ftrnn, frm n t fr."

8. "Mcky Mntl cn ht jst s gd rght-hndd s h cn lft-hndd. H's jst ntrlly mphbs."

9. "Y cn bsrv lt by wtchng."

10. " ddn't sy vrythng sd."

ANSWERS

1. "When you come to the fork in the road, take it."

2. "Ninety percent of the game is half mental."

3. "A nickel ain't worth a dime anymore."

4. "If people don't want to come out to the ball park, how are you gonna stop them?"

5. "Nobody goes to that restaurant anymore. It's too crowded."

6. "It gets late early out there."

7. "I took a two hour nap this afternoon, from one to four."

8. "Mickey Mantle can hit just as good right-handed as he can left-handed. He's just naturally amphibious."

9. "You can observe a lot by watching."

10. "I didn't say everything I said."

GAMES PEOPLE PLAY

What was the name of former U.S. president Richard Nixon's cocker spaniel?

Checkers.

THE NAME GAME

*Celebrities are famous for adopting stage names - Fred Austerlitz
changed his last name to Astaire, Susan Kerr Weld changed her first
name to Tuesday, and Wynette Pugh made her first name her surname
and changed her first name to Tammy. While the previously
mentioned names gave some hint of their alias, many of the famous
created monickers entirely different than their original name.
See if you can match those listed below.*

1. Elton John	a) Vincent Furnier
2. Charles Atlas	b) Maurice Joseph Micklewhite
3. Lucille Ball	c) Margaret Hyra
4. Alice Cooper	d) Annie May Bullock
5. Jason Alexander	e) Autlan de Navarro
6. Michael Caine	f) Angelo Siciliano
7. Lauren Bacall	g) Dianne Belmont
8. Carlos Santana	h) Betty Joan Perske
9. Tina Turner	i) Reginald Kenneth Dwight
10. Meg Ryan	j) Jay Scott Greenspan

ANSWERS

1. I.

2. F.

3. G.

4. A.

5. J.

6. B.

7. H.

8. E.

9. D.

10. C.

GAMES PEOPLE PLAY

Garnet Carter puttered around and made a small name
for himself when he invented what game in 1927?

Miniature golf.

I.Q. TEST

The above acronym, in this case, stands for "Initial Quotient." See if you can do O.K. by identifying what the following initials represent.

Now go to it A.S.A.P.

1. Tip (gratuity)

2. M.A.S.H. (infirmary)

3. Zip (code)

4. BVD (skivvies)

5. Scuba (diving)

6. EPCOT (amusement park)

7. STP (oil treatment)

8. FIAT (automobile)

9. Lasar (beam)

10. SOS (distress call)

GAMES PEOPLE PLAY

Charles Goren devised the point count bidding system
for what card game?

Bridge.

ANSWERS

1. To Insure Promptness.

2. Mobile Army Surgical Hospital.

3. Zoning Improvement Plan (as in Zip Code).

4. Bradley, Voorhees and Day.

5. Self-Contained Underwater Breathing Apparatus.

6. Experimental Prototype Community of Tomorrow.

7. Scientifically Treated Petroleum.

8. Fabricana Italiana Automobile Torino (Italian Automobile Factory at Torino).

9. Light Amplification by Stimulated Emission of Radiation.

10. Gotcha!!! SOS doesn't stand for anything. These letters were chosen as the Morse Code distress signal because of their simplicity: three dots, three dashes, three dots.

GAMES PEOPLE PLAY

What electronic game did Nolan Bushnell unveil in 1974?
Hint: It's a four-letter word.

Pong.

ROUNDABOUTS

What goes around, comes around, and this word association game challenges you to complete the circle in exactly five steps. Each word is associated with the words on either side of it. We've given you a letter in its proper position in each word. You may go either way.

Round 1 -

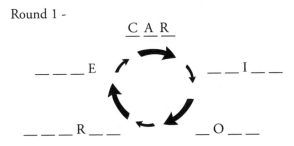

C A R

_ _ _ E

_ _ I _ _

_ _ _ R _ _

_ O _ _

Round 2 -

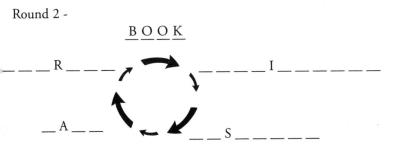

B O O K

_ _ R _ _ _

_ _ _ _ I _ _ _ _ _ _

_ A _ _

_ _ S _ _ _ _

ANSWERS

Round 1:   (Clockwise)

CAR, DRIVE, GOLF, COURSE, RACE

Round 2:   (Clockwise)

BOOK, APPOINTMENT, BUSINESS, CARD, LIBRARY

GAMES PEOPLE PLAY
(ON OTHER PEOPLE)

Don't expect a thumbs up with this one.
All you need is a full glass of water. Have a volunteer place
their thumbs together so that the tips touch the edge, not
the top, of a table or desk. Balance the glass of water on
their thumbs and watch the fun begin!

When at your favorite fast food place, specify that your
drive-through order is to go.

If you have access to two telephone lines and a friend who
has call waiting, this prank is a surefire winner. Call him/her
up and chat for a bit. Then, while you're talking, phone
their number again on the other line. They'll ask you to
hold on and then when they answer the call waiting line,
you'll be there! The fun doesn't end here. They'll come back
to the original line you dialed from and probably ask you to
continue holding. Play along and play it out!

SUM FUN

Sum fun for you. Fill in the blanks in such a way that the columns and rows add up to the number given at the right of the square.

_3_ _____ _____

_____ _____ _9_

_____ _8_ _____ = 20

_____ _____ _7_ _____

_____ _6_ _____ _____

_9_ _____ _____ _____

_____ _____ _5_ _____ = 27

_____ _____ _9_ _____

_____ _8_ _____ _____

_4_ _____ _____ _____

_____ _____ _____ _5_ = 30

ANSWERS

3	9	8
8	3	9
9	8	3 = 20

5	9	7	6
7	6	9	5
9	5	6	7
6	7	5	9 = 27

9	4	9	8
9	8	4	9
4	9	9	8
8	9	8	5 = 30

GAMES PEOPLE PLAY

It is the sixth note of the diatonic scale and is an acceptable two-letter word in Scrabble. Do you know it?

La.

POTPOURRI

1. If it's minus 40 degrees Fahrenheit, what's the temperature in Centigrade?

2. Fauntleroy is 100 percent honest. On the other hand, Fibber's name fits him to a tee. He can never tell the truth. One day one of them said, "The other one said he is Fibber." Which one said that?

3. Two words that begin with the letter "g" are spelled differently, yet mean the same thing. What are they?

4. If it takes the Seven Dwarfs seven days to dig seven holes, how long will it take one dwarf, Grumpy, to dig half a hole?

5. Left-out Lucy was born in the winter of 1984, yet her birthday is always in the summer and she's only four years old to this date. How come?

6. Three landscapers were raking leaves. One raked four piles of leaves in the front yard while the other two made eight piles in the backyard. When all the piles are combined, how many will they have?

7. In an ordinary deck of playing cards, how many eyes are on the four jacks?

8. A butcher, Mr. Miles is known as Montana's meat maven. He is six feet tall and wears a size eleven shoe. What does he weigh?

9. What day of the year is a military command?

10. What has a foot on each side and one in the middle?

ANSWERS

1. The same.

2. It had to be Fibber. If Fauntleroy had said it, that would mean it was a true statement, thus Fibber would have been telling the truth - and he never does.

3. Gray and grey.

4. A hole is a hole is a hole. There is no such thing as half a hole.

5. Lucy's birthday is in a place in the southern hemisphere that has a warm climate when North America is experiencing winter. She's only four years old because she was born in a leap year on February 29.

6. They will have one big pile of leaves.

7. Twelve ... There are two faces on each jack. Two jacks are one-eyed.

8. Meat.

9. March 4th.

10. A yardstick.

TRIVIQUATION

Test your math and your trivia wits here.
Fill in the number portion of the answers suggested by the clues
and then perform the arithmetic to solve the Triviquation.

1. Players on a lacrosse team   _____
2. White stripes on a U.S. flag*   - _____
3. Strings on a violin   x _____
4. Letters in Greek alphabet   - _____
5. Times Ford was elected U.S. President   = _____

*This has nothing to do with the above quiz, but since we're talking about the red, white and blue, let's run these questions up the flagpole and see if anyone salutes.

1. How many stripes did the U.S. flag have when Francis Scott Key wrote the Star Spangled Banner?

2. Destroying the American flag is frowned upon and is in some cases against the law, but what American hero was honored for doing so? Hint: Think North Pole.

3. An expert in the history of flags is a : a) piscatologist b) spermologist c) numismatist d) vexillologist

4. What do the terms "hoist" and "fly" refer to?

5. True or false? The flag's colors, red, white and blue, have no particular significance.

ANSWERS

1. 12

2. 6

3. 4

4. 24

5. 0

Now let's flag down the answers to the Old Glory quiz:

1. 15, which represented the amount of states at that time.

2. Robert Peary left pieces of the flag scattered at the North Pole.

3. D ... A piscatologist is a specialist in the study of fish; a numismatist is a coin expert; and a spermologist, believe it or not, is a trivia buff.

4. The hoist is the attached side of the flag while the fly is the body of it.

5. False ... Red stands for heartiness and valor; white symbolizes purity and innocence; and blue is for vigilance and perseverance.

MINDING YOUR P'S AND Q'S

The solutions to these clues all begin with p or q.

1. It's the first name of Columbo, the television detective played by Peter Falk.

2. Y.A. Tittle was one.

3. It has 119 ridges around it.

4. Remove the last four letters of this five-letter word and it's still pronounced the same.

5. A.C. Gilbert, the inventor of the erector set, scaled new heights when he won an Olympic gold medal in 1908 in this event.

6. Mythologically, she was the first mortal woman.

7. It's the airline to Australia.

8. Leon Uris wrote this book about a British libel trial.

9. This sport bans lefties.

10. A statue honoring this naval cartoon hero stands in Crystal City, Texas.

ANSWERS

1. Phillip.

2. A quarterback.

3. A quarter.

4. Queue.

5. The pole vault.

6. Pandora.

7. Qantas.

8. QBVII (which stands for Queens bench number 7, the court in which the trial takes place).

9. Polo.

10. Popeye.

GAMES PEOPLE PLAY

Tell everyone you're into buying pre-sliced bananas.
This fruity trick is accomplished by taking a
whole banana, inserting a fine needle through the
skin and levering it from side to side.
When the banana is unpeeled - presto! - pre-sliced pieces.

VERBAL VEXERS

What's the definition of ...?

1. alliaphage:
   a) a friend to a fault b) garlic-eater c) soapmaker d) bloodsucker

2. cardialgia:
   a) phobia of playing cards b) heartburn c) card deck minus jokers
   d) heartworm

3. dactylogram:
   a) measuring cup b) seed of the dactyl c) a quilt d) fingerprint

4. fulguration:
   a) bird-mating b) coffee-grinding c) lightning
   d) bathing in a hot tub

5. gracile:
   a) slender b) portulent c) kindly d) cowardly

6. jape:
   a) to daydream b) to dodge c) to play tricks d) to falsify

7. querimony:
   a) counterfeit currency b) an audit c) fake indentification
   d) a complaint

8. ranarium:
   a) an indoor track b) a frog farm c) public sauna bath
   d) incurable stutter

9. tetragram:
   a) a word with four letters b) head x-ray c) a plant that doesn't
   require sunlight d) a homing device for pigeons

10. vapulation:
    a) flogging b) itching c) scolding d) crying

ANSWERS

1. B.

2. B.

3. D.

4. C.

5. A.

6. C.

7. D.

8. B.

9. A.

10. A.

GAMES PEOPLE PLAY

What's the highest scoring three-letter word in Scrabble?

Zax.

WHAT NEXT?

*This game involves finding the common link of the series below
and then filling in what should follow.*

*Example: J,F,M,A,M,J,J,A,S,O,N, D - for December,
completing the series of the months of the year.*

1. Laura, Hillary, Barbara, Nancy, Rosalyn, Betty, Patricia, ...?

2. M,V, E, M, J, S, U, N, ...?

3. 6, 6, 7, 9, 8 , 6, ...?

4. A, K, Q, J, T, ...?

5. BN, SC, GL, RM, TD, ...?

6. S.A., J.P., J.C., ...?

7. Alpha, Bravo, Charlie, Delta, ...?

8. A, P, A, T, G, C, L, V, L, S, S, ...?

9. John, Michael, Terry, Graham, Eric, ...?

10. Brian, Dennis, Carl, Mike, ...?

ANSWERS

1. Lady Byrd (First Ladies).

2. P - Pluto.

3. 8 - The number of letters in the days of the week beginning with Sunday.

4. N - The descending order of cards.

5. PB - Pierce Brosnan ... They were all actors playing James Bond, not counting Casino Royale where almost everybody played him ... Barry Nelson (TV), Sean Connery, George Lazenby, Roger Moore, and Timothy Dalton.

6. J.L. - Jay Leno ... All were major hosts of *The Tonight Show.*

7. Echo ... These are the first five letters of the phonetic alphabet.

8. C - Capricorn (signs of the zodiac).

9. Terry Jones or Terry Gilliam, all members of *Monty Python.*

10. Alan (the original Beach Boys).

SPORTS SHORTS

Check out your sports smarts with these brain bafflers.

1. Quarterback Kurt Warner can hurl a football that would stop in mid-flight, reverse direction and then return to him. How does he manage this?

2. Is there better than a 50-50 chance that the next U.S. Tennis Open winner will have more than the average number of arms?

3. Football is doubly popular in this case. The Steelers and Eagles are two teams that have it; however, the Cowboys and Packers don't - and although the Lions had it first, the Bills have it twice. What is it?

4. A man left home one day and made three left turns. He then met a man wearing a mask. What was the first man's profession? And the second?

5. A football team had two star receivers named Moe and Larry. What was the quarterback's name.

6. A pitcher faced only 27 batters in a nine inning game, the minimum one could do. He struck out every batter. He allowed no hits and no runs yet his team lost 2-1. How could this happen?

7. Pigskin Pete, the prognosticator, claims he can tell the score of any football game before it even starts. How is it that he's always accurate?

8. Quarterback Tom Brady threw 25 passes in a game. All were incomplete, yet his passing percentage did not change. How come?

9. What's odd about each of the sports figures listed here?
Jimmie Fox   Tanya Harding   Wayne Gretsky

10. This one's a true story ... A horse named Cilohocla once made the circuit at Florida race tracks. Can you come up with a spirited reason why the stud was so named?

ANSWERS

1. He throws it straight up into the air.

2. Of course ... Since the average number of arms on a human is slightly less than two, anyone with two arms has more than the average.

3. The letter "l."

4. The first man was a baseball player. So was the second man - a catcher.

5. The quarterback's name was What (notice there's no question mark in the second sentence of the statement). Do you feel like a Stooge?

6. He was a relief pitcher.

7. Since the score of any football game before it starts is 0-0, Pete wouldn't have too tough a time zeroing in on it.

8. It was the first game of the season so Brady's percentage was .000 and it remained just that.

9. Their names are misspelled. The correct spellings are Jimmie Foxx, Wayne Gretzky and Tonya Harding.

10. Backwards, it spells "alcoholic."

WHICH IS IT?

1. Which three numbers give the same result when they are added as when they are multiplied?

2. Which are there more of: inches in a mile or Saturdays in a thousand years?

3. Which is longer: 250 centimeters or 8 feet?

4. Which animal has a greater life span: a rat or a cat?

5. Which are there more of: seconds in a week or feet in 100 miles?

6. Which is shorter: 666 days or 95 weeks?

7. Which weighs more: 3,600 ounces or 250 pounds?

8. Which is longer: a leap year or 8,760 hours?

9. Which is faster: 45 miles per hour or 72.42 kilometers?

10. Which is more: 76 gallons or 8,320 ounces of milk?

GAMES PEOPLE PLAY

What Japanese game company's name means "work hard, but in the end, it is in heaven's hands?"

Nintendo.

ANSWERS

1. The numbers 1, 2 and 3.

2. Inches in a mile equal 63,360 as opposed to Saturdays which total 52,000 and change (that change meaning leap year which will give it a bit of a boost depending upon which year and day you begin with).

3. 250 centimeters.

4. A cat (domestic) can live an average from 12 to 28 years while the average rat lives for four years.

5. Seconds in a week.

6. 95 weeks.

7. 250 pounds.

8. A leap year by 24 hours.

9. They're the same speed.

10. 76 gallons.

CHAT-CRONYMS

*Computer communicaton is about speed and people
communicating on the Web by using abbreviations
instead of typing out common expressions.
See how good you are at Net-speak
by deciphering the following acronyms.
Example: LOL - Laughing Out Loud*

1. TTFN

2. WB

3. YGBK

4. RBTL

5. OMIK

6. NAZ

7. LTNS

8. LTIC

9. GMTA

10. GAL

ANSWERS

1. TaTa for Now.

2. Welcome Back.

3. You Gotta Be Kidding.

4. Read Between The Lines.

5. Open Mouth Insert Keyboard.

6. Name Address Zip.

7. Long Time No See.

8. Laughing Till I Cry.

9. Great Minds Think Alike.

10. Get A Life.

GAMES PEOPLE PLAY
(ON OTHER PEOPLE)

This dastardly detergent deed ranks highly, especially since it involves our favorite room. Carve a lump of cheese into the shape of a bar of soap, put it next to the bath or shower and, well, you know the rest.

NICKNAME GAME

Test your geo-knowledge by matching these municipalities with their monikers.

1. City of Light	a) Lima
2. Athens of the North	b) Cape Town
3. City of a Thousand Spires	c) Odessa
4. Tavern of the Seas	d) Edinburgh
5. La Serenissima	e) Saigon
6. City of the Kings	f) Venice
7. The Eternal City	g) Marseilles
8. Paris of the Orient	h) Prague
9. Pearl of the Black Sea	i.) Paris
10. Queen of the Mediterranean	j) Rome

ANSWERS

1. I.

2. D.

3. H.

4. B.

5. F.

6. A.

7. J.

8. E.

9. C.

10. G.

GAMES PEOPLE PLAY

What are the playing tiles in Dominoes commonly called?

Bones.

TOM SWIFTIES

A "Tom Swiftie" is a kind of pun in which the verb or adverb plays off the setup. For example: "People don't need instructions to play a "Tom Swiftie" game," said Tom inexplicably. See how your sense of Tomfoolery stacks up.

1. "Pass the cards," said Tom _____.

2. "That power saw isn't very safe," said Tom _____.

3. "I'm about to hit the golf ball," Tom _____.

4. "We've got to make that typeface stand out more," said Tom _____.

5. "I bequeath," said Tom _____.

6. "Brothers," said Tom _____.

7. "I've got to fix the automobile," said Tom _____.

8. "You're burning the candle at both ends," said Tom _____.

9. "My grape juice has fermented," Tom _____.

10. "I just won one thousand dollars," said Tom _____.

ANSWERS

1. Ideally.

2. Offhandedly.

3. Forewarned.

4. Boldly.

5. Willingly.

6. Grimly.

7. Mechanically.

8. Wickedly.

9. Whined.

10. Grandly.

GAMES PEOPLE PLAY

What's the maximum number of squares a queen can move in the game of chess?

Seven.

PHONEY BUSINESS

*Companies often have telephone numbers in which the corresponding
letters on the keypad or dial spell out something indicative
of what they do. For instance, UPS has a number,
1-800-742-5877, which can also be dialed 1-800-PICK-UPS.
With this in mind, try to match the business
with the telephone number.*

1. Restaurant	a) 438-9675
2. Plumbers	b) 426-7873
3. Exterminators	c) 227-7855
4. Towing Service	d) 284-5455
5. Bakery	e) 227-9274
6. Dog Groomers	f) 328-9355
7. Auto Detailers	g) 738-2284
8. Employment Agency	h) 468-5282
9. Coffee Shop	i) 349-7473
10. Water Treatment	j) 468-6836

1	2 ABC	3 DEF
4 GHI	5 JKL	6 MNO
7 PQRS	8 TUV	9 WXYZ

ANSWERS

1. F ... E-A-T-W-E-L-L.

2. I ... F-I-X-P-I-P-E.

3. D ... B-U-G-K-I-L-L.

4. C ... C-A-R-P-U-L-L.

5. J ... H-O-T-O-V-E-N.

6. G ... P-E-T-B-A-T-H.

7. E ... C-A-R-W-A-S-H.

8. A ... G-E-T-W-O-R-K.

9. H ... H-O-T-J-A-V-A.

10. B ... H-2-O-P-U-R-E.

GAMES PEOPLE PLAY

Colonel Mustard is a suspect in what popular game?

Clue.

REALITY CHECK

*Identify which of the following places are real
and those which are simply legends.*

1. Timbuktu

2. Shangri-La

3. Transylvania

4. El Dorado

5. Camelot

6. Scotland Yard

7. Northwest Passage

8. Krakatoa

9. Mudville

10. Bermuda Triangle

GAMES PEOPLE PLAY

How many eyes are there in a 52-card deck?
(Hint: It's the same as the amount of dots on a pair of dice.)

ANSWERS

1. Real - a town in central Mali.

2. Legend - an imaginary island in the novel Lost Horizon.

3. Real - a region in Romania.

4. Legend - a fictional Spanish place which is loaded with gold.

5. Legend - the supposed English kingdom of King Arthur.

6. Real- the British law enforcement headquarters.

7. Real- sought for ages and finally discovered in the nineteenth century.

8. Real - at least until it blew itself up in a massive volcanic eruption.

9. Legend - fictional town for the epic poem *Casey at the Bat.*

10. It can be found on many maps but whether the goings-on there are real or not depends on whom you ask.

GAMES PEOPLE PLAY
(ON OTHER PEOPLE)

We're not advising this, but just imagine the fun it would be to stand on the side of the road and point a hair dryer at passing cars to see if they slow down.

THE SHAPE
OF THINGS TO COME

It's time to shape up or ship out.
Match the following shapely adjectives with their definitions.

1. Uniciform   a) grooved or depression-shaped

2. Guttiform   b) web-shaped

3. Eruciform   c) shaped like a drop of water

4. Sulciform   d) hand-shaped

5. Maniform   e) having holes like a sieve

6. Cribiform   f) caterpillar-shaped

7. Ensiform   g) sword-shaped

8. Falciform   h) shield-shaped

9. Scutiform   i) shaped like a hook

10. Textiform   j) sickle-shaped

GAMES PEOPLE PLAY

What are the three colors on a roulette wheel?

Black, green and red.

ANSWERS

1. I.

2. C.

3. F.

4. A.

5. D.

6. E.

7. G.

8. J.

9. H.

10. B.

GAMES PEOPLE PLAY

Do you know the American game which was introduced in 1867 after being adapted from the "Game of India?"

Parcheesi.

GAME BIRDS

*Here's a bit of indoor bird watching. See if you can spot
our feathered friends nested among these bird-brained clues.*

1. A loud-mouthed hoist.

2. Plays baseball in Canada.

3. A church official.

4. A muscular action of the throat.

5. Take a look.

6. The rear of a tent.

7. What peddlers do.

8. Totally insane.

9. Looks like a jaundice giraffe.

10. Plays the flute on the beach.

GAMES PEOPLE PLAY

This video game's name comes from a Japanese
mistranslation of King Kong. Can you name it?

Donkey Kong.

ANSWERS

1. Whooping Crane.

2. Blue Jay.

3. Cardinal.

4. Swallow.

5. Gander.

6. Canvasback.

7. Hawk.

8. Cuckoo or Loon.

9. Yellowthroat.

10. Sandpiper.

GAMES PEOPLE PLAY

Which has more squares, a checkers or chess game board?

They both have the same, 64.

OPPOSITES ATTRACT

These opposites have attracted so much that they've combined and need to be unscrambled.

For example: EHTLIFRTG is RIGHT/LEFT.

1. NRRUODEVE

2. FDOHSTRA

3. GTLIBLEIT

4. NRCTDILEYA

5. NPWUOD

6. OEMCOG

7. MTOTPBTOO

8. CITLHBWEKA

9. VEOOBBWALE

10. LEPFTMYLU

ANSWERS

1. UNDER/OVER.

2. SOFT/HARD.

3. BIG/LITTLE.

4. CLEAN/DIRTY.

5. UP/DOWN.

6. COME/GO.

7. TOP/BOTTOM.

8. BLACK/WHITE.

9. ABOVE/BELOW.

10. FULL/EMPTY.

GAMES PEOPLE PLAY

In some places it's known as "blind fly," in others,
"blind buck." What do we know it as here
in the good old U.S.A.?

Blindman's bluff.

MIXED BAG

1. I live in a house in which all the windows on all four sides face south. How is that possible?

2. If a brick weighs three pounds plus half a brick, how much does a brick and a half weigh?

3. What common element is expressed in the following letters? HIJKLMNO

4. There are 6 pears in a basket and 6 people in the room. How can you give each person a pear and still leave a pear in the basket?

5. How long would it take to boil 3 three-minute eggs?

6. Can you name the oldest settler in the west?

7. What is it that every man, no matter how meticulous or clever, always overlooks?

8. What is taken before you get it?

9. What men are always above board in their movements?

10. Add these numbers in your noggin: Begin with 1000. Add 40. Now add another 1000. Add 30. Now add another 1000. Add 20. Now add another 1000. Add 10. and your answer is …?

ANSWERS

1. The house is at the North Pole.

2. Nine pounds ... The brick weighs six pounds and half a brick weighs in at three pounds.

3. H2O.

4. You give the last person the whole basket, pear included.

5. Three minutes.

6. The sun.

7. His nose.

8. A picture.

9. Chessmen.

10. By any chance, did you get 5000? The correct answer is 4100.

GAMES PEOPLE PLAY

What video game derives from the Japanese word "Paka" (meaning "to eat")?

Pac-Man.

MARQUEE MANGLERS

*What's in a name? Plenty if it's a movie title.
Verbose is bad box office. See if you can recognize
the following blockbusters from these inflated titles.*

1. Pachyderm Personage

2. Vocalizing in the Atmospheric Condensation

3. Ruler of the Annuli

4. One Dozen Irritated Homo Sapiens

5. 200% Restitution

6. Celestial Orb of the Anthropoids

7. Expiring Arduously

8. That Which Occurred During the Anti-Solar Portion
of the Diurnal Cycle

9. Positioned Upon the Riparian Boundary

10. O Degrees by 315 Degrees True

ANSWERS

1. *Elephant Man.*

2. *Singing in the Rain.*

3. *Lord of the Rings.*

4. *Twelve Angry Men.*

5. *Double Indemnity.*

6. *Planet of the Apes.*

7. *Die Hard.*

8. *It Happened One Night.*

9. *On the Waterfront.*

10. *North by Northwest.*

GAMES PEOPLE PLAY

What are the six categories in Trivial Pursuit?

"Geography," "Entertainment," "Sports and Leisure," "History," "Art & Literature" and "Science & Nature."

IT'S THE SAME OLD SONG

See how you do in identifying the following juke box giants from these titles only a lawyer could love.

1. Pray Tell a Method of Ameliorating a Ruptured Muscular Hollow Organ?

2. A Less-Than-Favorable Natural Satellite in Ascension

3. Disembodied Apparition Eliminators

4. One More Complete Revolution of the Earth from Oklahoma's Second Largest City

5. Aggregates of H2O Constantly Descending Under the Influence of Gravity and Impacting My Cranium

6. Aureate-Dactyl

7. Ambulate in the Manner of an Inhabitant of the Valley of Kings

8. Maternal Parents, Dissuade Offspring from Maturing and Seeking Gainful Employment as Vaqueros

9. Benevolent Oscillations

10. What Individual Granted Freedom from Confinement to Members of the Genus Canis?

ANSWERS

1. *How Can You Mend a Broken Heart?*

2. *Bad Moon Rising.*

3. *Ghostbusters.*

4. *24 Hours from Tulsa.*

5. *Raindrops Keep Falling on My Head.*

6. *Goldfinger.*

7. *Walk Like an Egyptian.*

8. *Mamas, Don't Let Your Babies Grow Up to be Cowboys.*

9. *Good Vibrations.*

10. *Who Let the Dogs Out?*

GAMES PEOPLE PLAY

How many total properties would you find on a
Monopoly board?

28.

BY THE NUMBERS

1. What's the only number system where half of five is four?

2. There are 52 cards in a deck - four each of the ace, two, three, four, five six, seven, eight, nine, ten, jack, queen and king. What odd coincidence is there about the names of the cards?

3. How can you make six nines equal 100?

4. If you wrote down all the numbers from 1 to 100, how many times would the digit 4 appear?

5. What three-digit number is one-fifth of its original value if you lop off the first digit and then one-fifth of that value if you take away the second digit?

6. How many upper-case typewritten letters in the English alphabet are identical to their mirror image?

7. How much is half of 443,876 x 2?

8. The local historical society has leased Spivey Point Lighthouse to use as a museum. The original lease was 99 years. Two-thirds of the time past is equal to four-fifths of the time to come. How long until the lease runs out?

9. A man walked into a hardware store and was told that the items he wanted to purchase cost 25 cents apiece. He said, "I'll take 200." He was charged 75 cents. How can that be?

10. The last two numbers of the series below are 2 and 3. Your job is to place them in the correct order and determine why they're in that sequence.

    8   5   4   9   1   7   6   10   ?   ?

ANSWERS

1. Half of FIVE is "IV," four in Roman numerals.

2. The names spelled out collectively have exactly 52 letters!

3. 99 99/99

4. 20 - including 40, 41, etc.

5. 125.

6. 11.

7. Easy - 443,876.

8. 45 years.

9. He was buying house numbers.

10. 3, 2 … The numbers are in alphabetical order.

GAMES PEOPLE PLAY

How far apart are the stakes
in an official game of horseshoes?

40 feet.

SPEAKING IN TONGUES

*The English language has made common many foreign phrases.
See if you know the exact meaning to the following terms
and the land from which they were borrowed.*

1. C'est la vie

2. Quid pro quo

3. Potpourri

4. Carpo diem

5. Et cetera

6. Tempus fugit

7. Chutzpah

8. Que sera sera

9. E pluribus unum

10. Noblesse oblige

GAMES PEOPLE PLAY

How many marbles does each player get
to begin a game of Chinese Checkers?

10.

ANSWERS

1. French for "that's life."

2. Latin for "something in return."

3. French for "a mixture of things."

4. Latin for "seize the moment."

5. Latin for "and so on."

6. Latin for "time flies."

7. Yiddish for "brazenness."

8. Spanish for "what will be will be."

9. Latin for "one out of many."

10. French for "honorable and generous."

GAMES PEOPLE PLAY
(ON OTHER PEOPLE)

Here's a way to annoy someone. Tell them you know the
greatest knock-knock joke in the world and then begin,
"Knock-knock." "Who's there?" "Interrupting cow."
Just as they begin to say, "Interrupting …"
you interrupt them with a "moooooo."

TEAMING UP

Match up these famous duos.

1. Stanley	a) Guildenstern
2. Currier	b) Catherine
3. Quasimodo	c) Cleopatra
4. Rosencrantz	d) Napoleon
5. Anthony	e) Othello
6. Scarlett	f) Ives
7. Desdemona	g) Tristan
8. Heathcliff	h) Esmeralda
9. Isolde	i) Rhett
10. Josephine	j) Livingston

GAMES PEOPLE PLAY

What game would you be playing if you were using
the Nizmo-witch defense?

Chess.

ANSWERS

1. J.

2. F.

3. H.

4. A.

5. C.

6. I.

7. E.

8. B.

9. G.

10. D.

GAMES PEOPLE PLAY
(ON OTHER PEOPLE)

In the "cup runneth under" department: Get a styrofoam cup and punch a small hole in it near the base. Grasp the cup with a finger over the hole, fill it with water, then approach someone and ask them to hold the cup. At this point, you'd better make a run for it or you're liable to have more water on you than your victim.

PHRASE CRAZE PHASE II

*Once again, try to figure out the term
based upon the placement of the words.*

1. 1 2 3 4 5 6 7 8 9 0
   1 2 S A F E T Y 9 0
   1 2 3 4 5 6 7 8 9 0

6. I GOT   CALL
     GOT   CALL
     GOT
     GOT

2. LOFALLINGVE

7. SLEEPING
   THE JOB

3. JOANB

8. TENTGOODIONS

4. PACING
   GNICAP

9. STEP PETS PETS

5. COVER
   GOING

10. DDDWESTDDD

ANSWERS

1. Safety in numbers.

2. Falling in love.

3. An inside job.

4. Pacing back and forth.

5. Going undercover.

6. I forgot to call.

7. Sleeping on the job.

8. Good intentions.

9. One step forward, two steps back.

10. West Indies.

GAMES PEOPLE PLAY

What one word can you say in a roomful of sweet, little old ladies that can make them swear?

"Bingo!" (We hope you didn't take this one too seriously.)

CONNECTIONS-
CONNECTIONS-
CONNECTIONS

Fill in the blanks and connect the words below.

Example: fishing _____ cat becomes fishing pole cat

1. Red _____ stitch

2. Chocolate _____ condition

3. Thin _____ breaker

4. Easter _____ salad

5. Rocking _____ shoe

6. Jumping _____ knife

7. Butter _____ tape

8. Chevy _____ Gogh

9. Electric _____ card

10. Spare _____ West

ANSWERS

1. Cross.

2. Mint.

3. Ice.

4. Egg.

5. Horse.

6. Jack.

7. Scotch.

8. Van.

9. Charge.

10. Key.

GAMES PEOPLE PLAY

What mimicry game began in England as early as 1850
when it was known as Wiggle-Waggle?

Simon Says.

CHAIN LETTERS

In these puzzles, you must turn the first word into the second by changing one letter at a time and forming a new word at each stage.

1. Make FIRE produce HEAT:
   FIRE - ____ - ____ - ____ - ____ - HEAT

2. Change MICE into RATS:
   MICE - ____ - ____ - ____ - RATS

3. Obtain LOAN from BANK:
   BANK - ____ - ____ - ____ - ____ - LOAN

4. Turn SLEEP into DREAM:
   SLEEP - _____ - _____ - _____ - _____ - _____ - DREAM

5. Turn TEARS into SMILE:
   TEARS - _____ - _____ - _____ - _____ - _____ - SMILE

6. Make DEAD be LIVE:
   DEAD - ____ - ____ - ____ - ____ - ____ - LIVE

7. Put MILK into PAIL:
   MILK - ____ - ____ - ____ - PAIL

8. Evolve FISH into BIRD:
   FISH - ____ - ____ - ____ - ____ - BIRD

9. Turn OIL into GAS:
   OIL - ___ - ___ - ___ - ___ - GAS

10. Turn MORE into LESS:
    MORE - ____ - ____ - ____ - LESS

ANSWERS

1. FIRE - HIRE - HERE - HERD - HEAD - HEAT.

2. MICE - MITE - MATE - MATS - RATS.

3. BANK - BONK - BOOK - LOOK - LOON - LOAN.

4. SLEEP - BLEEP - BLEED - BREED - BREAD - DREAD - DREAM.

5. TEARS - SEARS - STARS - STARE - STALE - STILE - SMILE.

6. DEAD - LEAD - LEND - LENT - LINT - LINE - LIVE.

7. MILK - MILL - PILL - PALL - PAIL.

8. FISH - FIST - GIST - GIRT - GIRD - BIRD.

9. OIL - NIL - NIP - NAP - GAP - GAS.

10. MORE - LORE - LOSE - LOSS - LESS.

GAMES PEOPLE PLAY

How many ladders are there on a Chutes and Ladders board?

100.

MY WORD!

1. What do the following words have in common?
   screen inflammable dust left

2. Which of the following doesn't fit in with the rest?
   golf ball nail bargain bus table steer

3. This word is actually shorter when you add a syllable.
   What is it?

4. There are two words in this scramble of letters:
   OTDWRWSO. What are they?

5. What's the longest one-syllable word in the English language?

6. What's the shortest word that uses all five vowels?

7. What word is spelled improperly in every dictionary?

8. If you take the word "sparkling" and remove one letter,
   it will form a new word. Continue taking away one letter at
   a time to make new words until you are left with a single-
   letter word.

9. Somewhere in this sentence is a mispelled word. Can you
   find it?

10. What common word contains two E's, one W, one M,
    one C, one L and one other vowel?

ANSWERS

1. All have two different meanings.

2. Table ... You can "drive" everything else.

3. Short.

4. Two words.

5. Strengths.

6. Sequoia.

7. Improperly.

8. Sparkling, sparking, sparing, spring, sprig, prig, pig, pi, I.

9. The word is "misspelled" ... It should have two S's.

10. Welcome.

GAMES PEOPLE PLAY

Do you know the town in New Mexico
which was named after a TV game show?

Truth or Consequences.

NOUN SENSE

*See if you can come up with the noun
common to each set of words below.*

1. Black - score - chalk

2. TV - game - dog

3. Dish - train - television

4. Lottery - speeding - movie

5. Jingle - church - sleigh

6. Greeting - credit - report

7. Glasses - brow - patch

8. Stool - mother - ladder

9. One - drive - high

10. Welcome - auto - place

GAMES PEOPLE PLAY
(ON OTHER PEOPLE)

This is the "coin chicanery caper." Simply take a quarter,
glue it with some strong adhesive to a busy sidewalk and
watch the passersby try to pick it up.

ANSWERS

1. Board.

2. Show.

3. Set.

4. Ticket.

5. Bells.

6. Card.

7. Eye.

8. Step.

9. Way.

10. Mat.

GAMES PEOPLE PLAY
(ON OTHER PEOPLE)

If you want to telephone someone on their birthday, make it a real birthday call with this touch tone tune:

HAPPY BIRTHDAY

4	4	2	4	#	8	1	1	2	1	9	8
Hap-	py	birth-	day	to	you,	Hap-	py	birth-	day	to	you

INITIALLY SPEAKING, SECOND TIME AROUND

Once again, we ask you to determine what words will make these equations true.

1. 12 = E. in a D.

2. 3 = L. K. that L. T. M.

3. 57 = H.V.

4. 200 = D. for P. G. in M.

5. 29 = D. in F. (D. a L. Y.)

6. 7 = Y. of B. L. for B. a M.

7. 2 = H. are B. than O.

8. 1 = for A. and A. for O.

9. 7 = W. of the W.

10. 1492= C. S. the O. B.

ANSWERS

1. 12 eggs in a dozen.

2. 3 little kittens that lost their mittens.

3. 57 Heinz varieties.

4. 200 dollars for passing "Go" in Monopoly.

5. 29 days in February during a leap year.

6. 7 years of bad luck for breaking a mirror.

7. 2 heads are better than one.

8. 1 for all and all for one.

9. 7 wonders of the world.

10. 1492 Columbus sailed the ocean blue.

GAMES PEOPLE PLAY

In tiddlywinks, what's the name
of the piece flipped into the cup?

The wink.

TEEING IT UP

Basketball great Michael Jordan's burning interest for a multitude of sports is commonly known. His passion for baseball is such that he gave it a go as a career. No less is his fervor for the game of golf. And so, one day while visiting Pebble Beach, Jordan figured he'd make arrangements for an afternoon of play with one of the pros. As he perused the roster of participants in the upcoming golf charity tournament there, Jordan assessed what he thought might be their abilities against his undeniable talent. Jack Nicklaus, he felt, was out of the question. So was Lee Trevino. But, aha, Tiger Woods was making an appearance at the soon-to-be benefit outing! Jordan couldn't resist the opportunity to challenge the best of today's golfers. He asked and Tiger accepted.

It was a scorching afternoon when the pair met for their sporting affair. Indeed, the weather may have played a deciding factor in that the two wound up fairly evenly matched. The result: Tiger posted 70, Michael 78. There were no handicaps involved, yet Jordan was declared the winner. How come?

GAMES PEOPLE PLAY

In a poker game, what's known as the dead man's hand?

A pair of aces and eights as it's the hand Wild Bill Hickok was supposedly holding when he was murdered by Jack McCall.

ANSWER:

They were playing basketball, one on one.

GAMES PEOPLE PLAY
(ON OTHER PEOPLE)

Here are some quickies:

When the phone rings, answer it as if you're the caller. Say something like, "Hello is Egbert there?" This one really works well with telephone solicitors.

Give or lend a book-lover a novel and write the ending on the first page.

What a source of merriment it would be to build a snowman around a fire hydrant and watch the town bully try to kick it down.

This is an oldie but a goodie: Get a few people in on a joke that has no meaning at all and tell it to an unsuspecting victim. It could go like this: An elephant and a penguin are taking a bath together. The elephant says, "Pass the soap," and the penguin replies, "No soap, radio!" Everyone laughs and so might the victim! If not, they'll be scratching their head as to why they didn't get it.

Despite the pranksters that we are, we would never suggest replacing Oreos cookie cream with toothpaste.

NOTHING TO FEAR

Are you fearless when it comes to phobias?
See if you can match up these scares.

1. Autophobia
2. Harpaxophobia
3. Hippophobia
4. Bathmophobia
5. Xanthiphobia
6. Bogyphobia
7. Testophobia
8. Brontophobia
9. Anglophobia
10. Pantophoibia

a) fear of horses
b) fear of everything
c) fear of anything yellow
d) fear of tests
e) fear of being alone
f) fear of anything English
g) fear of being robbed
h) fear of demons and goblins
i) fear of walking
j) fear of thunderstorms

ANSWERS

1. E.

2. G.

3. A.

4. I.

5. C.

6. H.

7. D.

8. J.

9. F.

10. B.

GAMES PEOPLE PLAY

What yes-yes game derives from the
French and German affirmatives?

*The Ouija board. The name is a
combination of the French word for
yes, oui, and the German term, ja.*

HODGEPODGE

1. Name the phrase this represents: ON
                                  THE THE

2. In Hawaii, you can't take a picture of a man with a bald head. How come?

3. Is it physically possible for you to stand in front of someone and behind them at the same time?

4. What are the missing numbers?
   31 __ 31 __ 31 __ 31__ 30 ___ 30 __

5. Goldie was found dead in a puddle of water with broken glass. She had absolutely no cuts on her body. How did she die?

6. The fraction 24/31 is commonplace where?

7. If you divide 50 by a half and add 25, what's the answer?

8. What palindrome did Adam say to introduce himself to Eve?

9. What's the plural of mongoose?

10. Unscramble these cities and then identify which is the odd one out:
    STBONO   SCLOBUMU
    SUTINA   IPIHAEAPLDLH

ANSWERS

1. On the double.

2. You can't take a picture with a bald head anywhere. You need a camera.

3. Sure - if you stand back to back.

4. The numbers represent the days in each month of the year - 31 for January, 28 or 29 for February, 31 for March, etc.

5. A goldfish, she died of suffocation when the fishbowl was knocked over.

6. On a calendar.

7. 125 ... 50 divided by a half is 100, plus 25.

8. "Madam I'm Adam."

9. Mongooses.

10. Boston, Columbus, Austin, and Philadelphia ... The City of Brotherly Love is the odd one out because it's the only one that's not a state capital.

BOWL GAMES

*Last but not least, we offer these questions and teasers
about America's favorite reading room.*

1. Toilet paper was invented in 1857 by:
   a) Joseph Gayetty b) Mr. Whipple c) Arthur Scott
   d) Dred Scott

2. What did Francis I of France purchase in 1517 to hang in his
   bathroom?

3. Unscramble the bathroom-related terms below and then
   indentify the odd one out.
   HABTBUT HWEOSR ITETLO ORIRRM

4. Try to flush out the vowels which have been removed from
   this word: __ __ T H __ __ S __.

5. What does the following phrase represent?
   BATHREADINGROOM

6. See if you can figure out this bathroom graffiti item:
   IF PRO IS THE OPPOSITE OF CON, THEN PROGRESS...
   (Hint: Think government.)

7. What TV commercial made actress Jane Withers a star?

8. Fill in the consonants to complete this quote from comedian
   Morey Amsterdam: "I just bought a new house. It has no
   plumbing. It's u __ __ a __ __ __."

9. True or false? When John Quincy Adams became president
   (1825), the first toilet was installed in the White House and
   the throne soon became popularly known as the "Quincy."

10. Most toilet paper makers manufacture a sheet of paper which
    is 4 1/2 inches long. In an average 1,000 sheet roll, would
    there be enough toilet paper to go around the entire basepath
    of a big league baseball diamond?

ANSWERS

1. A.

2. *The Mona Lisa.*

3. Bathtub, shower, toilet and mirror ... Bathtub is the odd word out because all of the others are spelled with six letters.

4. Outhouse.

5. Reading in the bathroom.

6. PROGRESS IS THE OPPOSITE OF CONGRESS.

7. Maybe we should have said "made her a comet." Comet cleanser was the product that she endorsed as Josephine the Plumber.

8. Uncanny.

9. True.

10. Yes ... 375 feet of toilet paper does the job with 15 feet to spare.